On the S

Written by Jo Windsor

Rigby

Here is a shell.

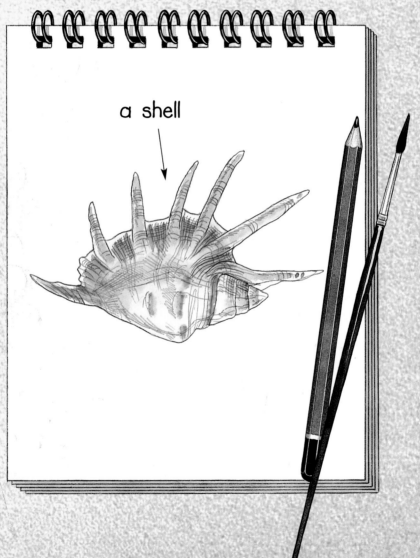

a shell

Here is a crab.

a claw

Here is a seagull.

a beak

Here is a turtle.

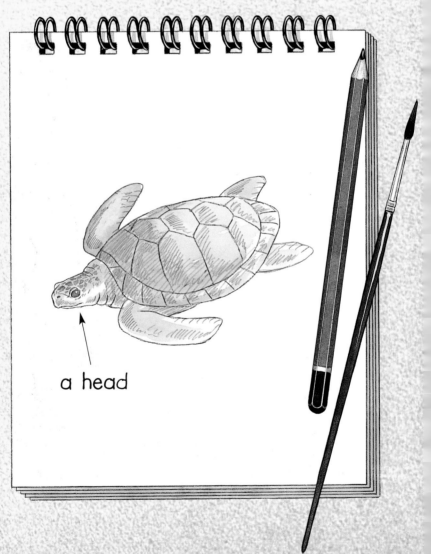

a head

Here is a pelican.

a foot

Here is a seal.

a flipper

Index

crab 4-5

pelican . . . 10-11

seagull 6-7

seal 12-13

shell 2-3

turtle 8-9

Guide Notes

Title: On the Seashore

Stage: Emergent – Magenta

Genre: Nonfiction (Expository)

Approach: Guided Reading

Processes: Thinking Critically, Exploring Language, Processing Information

Written and Visual Focus: Photographs (static images), Illustrations, Index

Word Count: 24

READING THE TEXT

Tell the children that this book is about some animals that live on the seashore.

Talk to them about what is on the front cover. Read the title and the author.

Focus the children's attention on the index and talk about the animals that are in this book.

"Walk" through the book, focusing on the photographs and talk about the different animals.

Read the text together.

THINKING CRITICALLY

(sample questions)

*   What other things can live on the seashore?
*   Why do the animals in this book live on the seashore?

EXPLORING LANGUAGE

(ideas for selection)

Terminology

Title, cover, author, photographs, illustrations

Vocabulary

Interest words: seashore, crab, shell, seagull, turtle, pelican, seal
High-frequency words: here, is, a